But….. My Hair Isn't Done!!

By: Veleta J.

BUT...... MY HAIR ISN'T DONE!!

But....My Hair Isn't Done!
©2018 Veleta Y. Jones

Printed in the United States of America

The views expressed in this manuscript are solely the opinions of the Author.

The author has represented and warranted full ownership and/or legal rights to publish all the materials in this book.

This book may not be reproduced or transmitted for commercial or non-commercial use in any form which includes but not limited to photocopying, electronic or mechanical recording without the Author's written approval.

Published by:
Veleta Y. Jones in association with Author Tanisha D. Mackin, LLC

BUT…… MY HAIR ISN'T DONE!!

"You have just stepped into a fearless territory"

I WROTE THIS BOOK IN A COMPLETE STATE OF WRITERS BLOCK…LOL

But thank you for picking this book up because you think the cover is dope right?! Consider your **CONFIDENCE** flawless after you read this though.

Veleta J.

BUT…… MY HAIR ISN'T DONE!!

THANK YOU GOD FOR CHOOSING ME. MY GOAL IS TO GET TO THE OTHER SIDE TO SEE YOU ONE DAY.

THANK YOU TO MY SUPPORTERS WHETHER IT IS FAMILY OR FRIENDS -MY APPRECIATION IS SINCERELY GENUINE.

BUT…… MY HAIR ISN'T DONE!!

APPETIZER

YOU HAVE WAITED LONG ENOUGH FOR THAT BLESSING TO COME IN THE MAIL BUT CAN'T EVEN GO TO THE MAILBOX BECAUSE YOUR HAIR IS NOT DONE. SOME OF YOUR PALS HAVE PLANNED A NIGHT OUT, BUT YOU CANCELLED BECAUSE YOU DON'T KNOW WHAT TO DO WITH YOUR HAIR. YOU DIDN'T POST THAT INSPIRATIONAL VIDEO ON SOCIAL MEDIA BECAUSE YOUR HAIR WASN'T CUTE IN YOUR EYES. MOST PEOPLE WILL VIEW THESE AS THE NEED TO BE CLASSY OR NEVER BE CAUGHT WITH YOUR HAIR UNDONE MOMENTS, BUT THE PROBLEM IS YOUR FEAR OF WHAT

BUT…… MY HAIR ISN'T DONE!!

OTHERS THINK AND HOW THEY FEEL ABOUT YOU. THE COMMON DENOMINATOR CONSIST OF YOU NOT BEING CONFIDENT ENOUGH. IT'S SIMPLY YOUR FAULT FOR ALLOWING THEM TO BOX YOU IN WHEN THERE WAS NEVER A BOX TO BEGIN WITH.

THIS PAGE TURNER WILL HELP YOU LIVE A LIFE OF NO EXCUSES AND LEARN 6 TURN KEY LIFE HABITS THAT WILL BOOST YOUR CONFIDENCE TO THE TUNE OF ONE MILLION NOTCHES…SO, THIS IS NOT ABOUT HAVING TO MAKE HAIR APPOINTMENTS, BUT LIVING A LIFE OF URGENCY WHEN IT COMES TO BEING CONFIDENT IN EVERYTHING

BUT…… MY HAIR ISN'T DONE!!

THAT YOU ARE AND EVERYTHING THAT YOU WILL BECOME. NOW GO AND LIVE THE LIFE THAT COMMANDS GREATNESS FROM THE UNIVERSE.

BUT…… MY HAIR ISN'T DONE!!

The Menu

APPETIZER…………………………… 6

ENTRE

Chapter 1-Highlights…………………….. 10

Chapter 2- Deep Condition……………..... 17

Chapter 3- Trim……………………….. 24

Chapter 4-New Growth……………….. 35

Chapter 5- Touch-up…………………... 47

Chapter 6- The big chop……………….. 61

From the Author's desk……………..….. 71

BUT…… MY HAIR ISN'T DONE!!

A flower does not fear the other flower next to it because it just blooms

"Author Unknown"

Chapter 1 – Highlights

Affirmation: I am a winner!

Remember the day before you were born? Can you remember the day you were born? Can you remember the day after you were born? Can you even explain why you can't remember those days? My point exactly…do you need those details to be the best you that you possibly can be? The popular saying goes" The two most important days in your life is the day you were born and when you find out why. The shadow that you may walk in is merely an uncolored version of you.

It is time to operate outside of the box that doesn't even exist. It's easy to blame what you think is a failure on GOD. The path God has planned for our lives is already set in stone. It is safe to subtract the hundreds of detours that we cause in a lifetime. We look at struggles as negative factors in our lives. Therefore, the common denominator would ultimately be for you to give up, right? Wrong, because life has a way of making a crazy situation in your life anti-up your confidence. Situations have expiration dates which makes it even more beautiful. Needing to know every little detail of every little thing can make you go crazy. So, don't be like me and need to know the end dates of stuff, even though it may not even happen. No one wants to look stupid so don't go after your goals and aspirations, right?

Back to square one-the root problem is our attempt to impress others and live up to your neighbor's standards; while the whole time they admire you in secret. There will always be things that try to come against you, but here is what you must realize...there is also good things pushing the bad things out of the

BUT…… MY HAIR ISN'T DONE!!

way. I simply say that God's angels are working on your behalf and others may say it's the Universe…when GOD is the one that created the Universe. Stop thinking that it's a higher power and just say the name GOD because he is the one that knew you before you were in your mother's womb… I thought you knew!!! The thought of you being left to fend for yourself is probably your current state of mind and it keeps haunting you day in and day out. No one listens to you, no one listened to you, and no one cried with you. Well you weren't necessarily born to be in the in-crowd nor were you born to be average so what makes you think you must look, smell, talk, think, and act like everyone else? Someone told me a few months ago that I am cocky, then they changed it to saying that I am too confident. I didn't respond with anger at all. This individual compared me to the Mayweather's recent opponent, Mcgregor. I was compared to

BUT...... MY HAIR ISN'T DONE!!

Mcgregor during the fight. To say the least I was impressed that this person saw me in this light. I was not shocked; in all that I do I bring my A game with confidence.

I have good reasons to be confident. Not only because God wants me to be confident, but when I was about 12 years old, I entered a talent show contest with 2 other girls performing "Hold on" by the famous R&B duo group EnVogue. Prior to signing up we all agreed that we were going to go through with it because that's what we consistently rehearsed for. On the day of the talent show both girls chickened out. I ended up performing a group song with just me. As I think back to that moment 20 years later I understand now that that moment was to push me into getting over a fear of being in front of an audience. The other 2 girls commended me on performing. Even though I lost the talent show I was still a winner for not quitting on myself. I can think of so many "Why me" moments in my life until I am blue in the face. For example, it always crosses my mind from time to time how hurt I was from past relationships. All those things happened to mold me, and to break me out of my comfort zone. Pain does not last forever. There are at least one to five people waiting for you to Glow-up. On the other hand, there are some people possibly waiting for your downfall. You don't have to worry about the ones waiting on your downfall because God is handing out so many chairs for them to have a seat. Have you ever run into someone and they asked you why haven't you accomplished this? Or why haven't you accomplished that? Then you're wondering why their finite brains are even worried about your goals or if even that is still your goal to begin with.

Just because you are not on the big screen or don't have 171k followers on social media does not mean you are not changing a life or being an impact to someone else. Most of the time it is the person that will not publicly recognize you, but silently praise you. You see, things have to happen in order to show that there is a God, right? Hardships have to happen in order to have a positive outcome, so why not be the person to endure long suffering and tell your story? Do I still go through things? Of course. Do I still question God? Of course. Do I have opportunity days? Of course. Do I want to give up and pass the torch to someone who I think is stronger or can handle what I think I can't? Um…. yes, to all of these.

Looking back over your life… you have come this far. That last situation you didn't think you were going to get over. You did.

Beliefs become thoughts...thoughts become words...words become actions... actions can simply start a movement.

Being confident starts in the mind first.

☺ Godly. Happy. Positive. Wise. Free.

☹ Mad. Envious. Depressed. Boastful. Negative

Chapter 2-Deep Condition

Affirmation: I am open minded..

In life, there are a lot of things that can hit us all at one time, and we take a lot of unnecessary time trying to correct the things on the surface. Fixing the outer things can lead to self-destruction. You lost a job because you were not performing. You go apply for another job and another job and another job never fixing the fact of matter of the need to increase your skillset. Not a single job has called you back yet. There could be other reasons beyond your control of not being hired right away at another job, but the common denominator here is enhancing your skillset. This could be taking free online courses, enrolling in college, learning from other successful people, enlisting the help of a mentor... now we think of a mentor as a free service, but you can't put a price on the power of a mentor...so there could be a fee for mentoring services; this is case by case. On a personal note. Case in point-my former job closed without notice.

My thoughts: Living in the state of Ga, this state has an at-will employment policy where I can quit when I feel the need and the employer can let me go when they feel the need. I admit I was deep in thought trying to figure out my next move. I have been an entrepreneur ever since 2013, and I knew in my heart I truly wanted to be a work at home boss not taking orders from someone else. Now God will always sit on the throne and my fear of God will always keep me on my toes.

I then said to myself, "I can do one or two or three things. I can look for another job, sit back and pout, worry myself crazy, or boss up and level up on my skills". I finished college with a 4-year Bachelor's degree with a concentration in Human Resource Management, wrote another book, started blogging, started networking more, built my own website, and started my own confident community called "Konfident Chix. This global organization uplifts and brings the boldness out of anyone while helping them level up in their confidence.

    I did all this even while still looking for another job. Why did I look for another job? I wanted some in between money for the days where my business did not make money. Holding the mommy hat keeps my mind on safe mode constantly. Even though playing it safe can seemingly be stereotyped for average people, I believe it is a case-by-case for any one. Investing in yourself is the best investment you will ever make in your life. You will be set up though for frustration, because anything that you are connected to primarily means you played a part in it if things don't go your way. What comes to mind when something is deep conditioned? Getting rid of toxins, dirt and even changing the familiarity up all together.

Conditioning the entire you should always be at the top of your bucket list. If nothing is ever cleared out for new things to come in…chaos will take its course. Want a new car but your car is never cleaned, want a new home but its pack racked and never clean, want new friends but you talk about the ones you have and never smile, want new clothes but don't take care of the clothes you have, want your income to increase but you have thoughts of lack and you want a new career, but you treat your current one like it's not a blessing. I am far from perfect.

You see I had to do a deep condition in my life to even write this book. At first, I wanted to hire a Ghostwriter but this book is from the bottom of my soul and I wanted to personally write it. Everyone is a work in progress. Someone said to me the other day "Girl you made it". I said no I have not made it yet. She then proceeded ... you have a book, a business, blah blah blah. Some people see the end results, but haven't walked through the actual journey. New condition and re-condition fall into many categories. Re-condition just simply refers to reprogramming your mind to do what is used to do. I believe the hardest thing for some people to do is re- condition their minds. It is by far the most important element we can control. I gave up writing books at one point. My mind was conditioned to think I was finished writing books. On the flip side when God puts a call on your life it's truly hard to stay away from it.

BUT…… MY HAIR ISN'T DONE!!

My mind set is…since changing lives is ongoing for me, quitting is not an option. I watch my daughter closely because I see her mind is telling her to go get the ball, go get her juice cup, go get her toy. I think it is cute by the way. As adulthood sets in, we start associating with people that is conditioned to things differently than how we do things. Not to say they do things wrong, but they may see a need to do it a certain way. For example, there is a movie where a group of guys stole for a living. To them, they had a good thing going. They were done with the thieving life until a bad seed came back to the group to make a proposition. The proposition was to take on one more job that could bring in up to $6 million dollars apiece. It sounded good to everyone even though a couple of them has some reservations about it. The job didn't go so well because the bad seed didn't tell them his own personal plot underneath the surface. Lives were lost, the

BUT…… MY HAIR ISN'T DONE!!

hate became more intense, and the greed was a killer basically. Some didn't make it to the end and some walked away with a lot of cash. Moral of the story, if the group would have deep conditioned their minds they would have got the money the honest way.

They also would have declined the offer from the bad seed. The bad seed was the type of person that schemed and plotted to cover their own butt. Funny how the rest of the group knew that but failed to acknowledge it.

Chapter 3-Trim

Affirmation: I am organized

I mentioned earlier that this book is not about salon visits, but have you ever got your hair trimmed, and when you look at all the hair on the floor you started wanting the old hair back immediately. Why do you think that is? Well for starters it could be that you never wanted your hair trimmed to begin with. That is how we are when it's time to clean house in our own lives. Think of it as a blessing to narrow things in your life down just a notch. This is a major benefit to boosting confidence because overloads in a person life is clutter.

What can you find through clutter? Things out of order. Every time I make a purchase whether it is for a car, a TV, or even a pot set I always trim my options down to the top three items then make a choice from there.

BUT…… MY HAIR ISN'T DONE!!

My first option is brand and what makes them different. My second option is quality of the product then finally I go by price. Remember the time you were looking for something and found something else instead? That something else is what you were looking for before. I remember when I was looking for a receipt for an item I purchased and found $10.00 in another purse. I was excited, but I begin to think that if I TRIM some things down and get rid of some stuff in my handbags… I can find what I am looking for.

Isn't that how life is? There are so many that want to be popular but end up adding people that don't mean them any good. So, what they ended up doing is adding dead ends to the highlight of their life. In a particular movie I remember in a scene someone said "Please trim that fat or she will kill me". He meant kill because his wife would literally hate him for not trimming the hideous fat off her juicy meat. I think it is the thought of the fat being on there. Then the wife obviously wanted to control her spouse in that movie.

Dead weight can have a happy ending if somethings are trimmed from it. The first thing that might come to the mind when talking about dead weight is being the opposite of skinny. Not in this sense. No No No...things weighing your mind down. Did you know that saying a simple hello to a total stranger adds energy to your nervous system? I am not in the medical field, but what can a person loose by simply speaking to someone? I recently shared in a blog post of mines how to declutter your life when going into the fall season. Have you ever wondered why in a years' time there are four seasons? They begin then they end; it is a repeated cycle. This will never change, but it is meant to spark a trim in your life to make changes at the end of every season.

When going into your next season, try to avoid a season that has too much going on in it. Prioritizing is a very important factor. I am pretty sure you have heard of six degrees of separation, right? So, then you should understand that if nothing is ever trimmed out of your life then the very thing that you are seeking may get overlooked because again it is too much clutter in your pathway.

Every living being on this earth is five people away from being effectively connected to the very thing that can make you a millionaire. For example, my favorite actor is Regina Hall. If I really pressed the issue of meeting her I am effectively five folks away from actually locking shoulders with her.

BUT...... MY HAIR ISN'T DONE!!

Have you ever noticed in movies everything starts off good then somewhere in between they allow people or things to get on their train which was meant to never stop, and give instructions outside of the life God has planned for them, then once they come back to reality things are good again in some cases? For example, there is a movie where a couple gets married suddenly and money was never an issue, but the wife started noticing weird behavior of her new husband. She remembered asking him questions about his past because he never talk about his family much. His usual answer is "I was adopted and never knew my real family."

One day the wife explained to her husband she wanted to start a career and to not be a home wife, but a wife that supports the house financially as well. Her husband became so angry and yelled at her for assuming she wants to leave him and she does not love him anymore. The wife was so stunned by her husband's response and was confused by him not being supportive. Days went by before her husband spoke to her, and he ignored her like she wasn't even there. The wife decided to do some digging on her husband's past. She found out that her husband was accused of killing his own mother when he was in high school. She became frantic because the research showed that his mother died of a fall from the top of the stairs. It conveyed that someone pushed her, but it was not enough evidence to prove that. She then started to wonder why her husband kept this from her.

Moral of this story is, she married very quickly and her need to be with a man caused her to marry a person she hardly knew anything about. In life, if we know the things that deeply saddens us and we leave them not attended to, it can cause us to miss out on opportunities and or get involved with or have relationships with people that are not on the trail of our destiny.

Trimming desires down that we know are not good for us or we know that does not serve us any justice can even be one step closer to mental healing. I am not talking about wanting to be a millionaire or wanting a new tesla or wanting to travel the world. The underlying factor are your true motives behind the things you desire. What comes to your mind when you think of the word trim? My mind goes directly to someone doing gardening and trimming hedges on a sunny day.

I for one never really been the gardening type, but I am open to it. If nothing is ever trimmed down in your life sometimes God may hold what is for you for a little while for your own good. Often times our minds think that adding a middle man to a situation can fix some things.

    I remember when my husband and I moved into our new home, we knew nothing about being a homeowner, so we didn't get the seller to add the electronic garage opener to the closing list. We decided to go to a local hardware store and get the garage opener to attempt to install it ourselves.

    Upon doing that a worker asked us if we needed help, and that he installs garage openers on the side. So, we agreed for him to come over and do our garage. To make a long story short we ended up paying extra to repair what the hardware store worker messed up because he didn't install it properly. We hired a professional to remove what the first guy did and install it the right way.

BUT...... MY HAIR ISN'T DONE!!

In this case it was necessary to allow our minds to weed out the grand idea that adding a middle man to do our garage would solve the issue of it getting done the right way the first time. Ever since I have been doing the adult thing, anytime I make a purchase or get a service done I always use the 3-rule lifesaver.

This is a for sure satisfaction guarantee of liking the product or service. I choose the top 3 best providers or products then I look at the reviews, and after that I research the quality of the product. Then I move on to the best deal or I decide is it worth the cost. This rule has saved me thousands of dollars and saved me time as well. On another note trimming down your list of things to do can help increase your life tremendously. I used to give myself a ton of things to get done in one day. One day I grew tired of having to get so much done. I then grew fond of time management and telling people no when I truly did not have the time to get the task done. I read in an article one day that a celebrity was rushed to the hospital due to lack of rest and dehydration.

      I begin to think to myself if this person ever took time to enjoy the fruits of their loins without having to sacrifice sleep and rest. I know hard work is key when things need to get done, but the bottom line is saying yes to everything can cost more than you bargained for. Did you know that trimming things down in your life can cause new growth to be attracted to your life? Today going forward consider your life trimmed to the size that is suitable for you to handle.

BUT…… MY HAIR ISN'T DONE!!

Think of the top 3 things you would be better off with if you went without it

"Everything starts with a thought".
~Author Unknown~

Chapter 4-New Growth

Affirmation: I am Confident

New growth can fall in so many categories, but my all-time favorite is the art of personal growth and development. Did you know that some people are not aware that they can grow? Anyone can grow from unhealthy situations, grow out of stale relationships and outgrow old habits and develop new ones. There are a lot of people in the world who suffer from habits that weigh them down, and it can be so hard to grow out of it.

In this case, you must give yourself permission to grow and ask GOD to help you focus on other things other than the habit itself. For example, I recently started getting my nails back done because I used to bite them every so often. Some people call it a nervous condition I called it being hungry. Either way it was a habit I knew I wanted to break.

Often times, a lot of people don't want to grow because they fear losing people in their lives or they fear change. The common thing about this is we all have something we fear. But I believe it is time to channel that fear and do something our future self will thank us for.

I remember my daughter was born weighing less than 5 pounds; the same as my baby weight. She was a nice size to me and beautiful in my eyes. It was something about her that allowed me to look past her actual size and look into her eyes. I knew at that very moment she will accomplish great things in her life. I know she would make me and her father proud. Since my Minnie me is on the petite side, whenever anyone saw her they would first mention that she is so small. I guess they were

BUT…… MY HAIR ISN'T DONE!!

comparing her to other babies because she fit perfectly in her sized clothing.

Nevertheless, before my eyes she is getting so big and that's when the demands will come. People will grow at their own pace. Most of the time life situations will cause you to grow up quicker than you intend to. Believe it or not I have been put in many situations that caused me to grow up quicker than I intended to. I am pretty sure we have all been in scary situations that we wish we could magically reverse in an instant.

The popular phrase "Go zero to one hundred really quick "is very popular and I lived that phrase for a short period of time because I was ordered to do 40 hours of community service, which I hated by the way. They gave us a list of places we can choose from, but supervising at a bank I was working at demanded me to be at work a lot.

At first, I ended up going to a local community service place where we would have to pick up trash outside in the rain. It was so funny because I ended up leaving before the lead person gave the instruction. My final destination ended up cleaning a clean gym. "Won't God do it" was all I can say in my mind. The craziest part of this thing called "Life".

There will always be a person assigned to your destiny that will cause you to change in certain areas of your life. I say that because I was assigned to a lady that gave me a hard time in community service about how my disposition was when holding a mop. My thoughts were "I have been mopping for years" How dare you ask me if I ever mopped before because I wasn't holding the mop like you thought I should.

BUT…… MY HAIR ISN'T DONE!!

Sounds crazy, right? This went on for about 6 weeks. I was only assigned 40 hours, but it felt like forever.

Let me back up a few sentences. The community service I did helped me become more patient with people.
So now it is time put our big pants on. There will be times of uncertainty and fear factors because it can be uncomfortable to come out of time in your life where the things that you are used to doing has to have a new routine in order to grow. I recently shared in a blog on my site kisforkonfident.online highlighting that I received a small plant from my neighbor just because.

This was so nice of her to think of me. At first, I was thinking this is something else for me to look after and take care of. But then it hit me along the lines of growth. It's one of those indoor and outdoor plants. Of course, it will need sunlight and water every day. I also shared on my blog that I was in a season of receiving all the good in my life. The plant represents overflow to me. In order for new growth to properly grow...the old outdated stuff needs to be cut like withered grass.

    Sometimes the feeling of being stuck in a particular issue or particular season can cause someone to really lose sight of the very thing that is waving you down. Just recently I was in a season that seemed like lack. Lack in the form of feeling like I didn't have enough.

    Enough of what? Friends? Invitations? Money? Happy days? Book sales? Book sales. In life it seems when you have more you start eventually wanting more. A popular saying of "When you have more money you have more problems", brings me to the thought of others

BUT…… MY HAIR ISN'T DONE!!

desiring something someone else has only to find out how they obtained it, and now it becomes a turn off.

Someone asked me to be their life mentor out the blue one day. Their reason was because I seem to have it all, know it all, and have everything good going for me. I said honey let me tell you this. "I have had my share of ups and downs even more downs than ups. It's how I learned to coast through life. God had to literally shake me to learn how to get from one season to the next. It is not that I have everything because the things I have a desire to accomplish in my eyes I haven't hit the finish line yet.

I begin to tell this individual I spent a few years really being at a low point and it was quite embarrassing because I am known to be bubbly, funny, and the life of the party as I have

BUT…… MY HAIR ISN'T DONE!!

heard others say that about me. I have always felt I wasn't photogenic, so I never wanted to be in photos or especially take photos of myself. It always seemed as though I looked like someone else in photos and not who I really am. To combat this feeling, I finally scheduled my first photo shoot and it was very nice.

This is another example of how I welcomed new growth in my life. I did this not because of other people, but because those photos actually help to dig deep, and they helped me discover the real me and increase my level of confidence. During my shoot I also got a sense of other attributes dealing with my personality.

I must admit that after my session I felt empowered even more to take on anything that comes my way, and execute any idea that God gives me. Doing things that are unheard of benefits anyone by enhancing their dexterity and social independence. Have you ever wondered that most things whether is a marriage, new market product, plant, adulting functions better after it has grown to another level?

For example, it seems like every holiday a new phone hits the market and they sell like crazy for the first wave then eventually the sales decrease because the kinks are still being worked out? Therefore, potential buyers are waiting on the complaints or compliments to roll in before they buy the product.

In a nutshell, following the crowd is going backwards in life. There is nothing wrong with supporting the dreams of others, but you must put your mask on first to help others. I grew up in many small towns so people did what others did for the most part simply because a set vision was not implemented. Operating from many hats I am always presented with ways to grow and mature. The ones that make me feel uncomfortable allows me to see things more clearly because I am usually in a state of always wanting to improve in self-development.

A person that is aware of what is going on around them is focused and passionate about growing to another level which is why coaches need coaches, leaders need a team behind them, and most of all God's guidance.

I lived on my own at a very early age and to be honest I am certain that it was only God leading me because as I look back over my life I have no idea how I knew what next move to make. It almost seems unbelievable that I had two jobs, a car, a roommate, and a bank account all before the age of 20.

BUT…… MY HAIR ISN'T DONE!!

I am far from perfect which is why I was as brave as my younger self to do the impossible. These days are filled with putting gratification first instead of dealing with pain first. Putting pain first shows self-control in so many ways. As the late Whitney Houston said it best "It is easy to give into our fears". You have a choice to mature and for that it is one of the most priceless moments in your life.

Think of three things that need to grow in your life and find ways work toward them.

"You must be the change you wish to see in the world"
~Mohatma Gandhi~

Chapter 5- Touch up

Affirmation: I am a positive person

`In my early twenties, I was diagnosed with endometriosis, female condition where the tissues lay outside the endometrial tissue causing constant pelvic pain. Without even knowing I had it, I went to the doctor for a regular checkup and found out about it then. I didn't take it hard at all. I don't know why maybe because sometimes in our youth a lot of things go over our heads. I decided to have an injectional procedure which allows the endometriosis to go away. The doctor said it will be hard for me to have kids or I will never be able to have kids. I do know anything is possible for those that have faith and believe in GOD.

At one point in my life I didn't believe that I could really control my thoughts. I know

BUT…… MY HAIR ISN'T DONE!!

that sounds crazy but I honestly felt like I could not control my thoughts to be positive which would eventually lead me into having positive words and energy. Since I have a vivid imagination anyways I came to a bridge that I had to cross that lead me to having a desire for detoxing my mind. We all have something that we don't want to face in life. That is nothing to be ashamed of. Touching up the things in your life that can make your life better is one of the best gifts you can give yourself.

For instance, if a book is bought and never read how you would expect to learn from the book or better yet, what if you have never conditioned your mind to say daily affirmations. Whatever you say about yourself good or bad you are right because your words have power. I remember when I hit my late twenties going into my early thirties I had so much doubt that doubt got tired of me. I literally used to doubt everything and expected the worst things to happen. I must admit my life hasn't always been an elevator ride. For example, I remember when I felt my life was over when I gave birth to my daughter.

Don't get me wrong she is an absolute blessing to me, but in my mind, I felt as though I haven't achieved my dreams because of this thing called time. There were never enough hours in a day until I made it a priority to include time management, even before my day starts. I even went so far as to planning my entire week out on Sunday so I can prioritize and identify what urgently needed my attention now and what can actually wait.

When a person's life seems overloaded more than likely they have too much on their plate and the word no, might make them feel bad if they use it. I made a pact with myself that there is not one person on this earth that can pull me out of the bed unless it is an emergency. This is simply valuing my time and getting the proper sleep. Most things can wait until morning to get worked out.

Alleviating concerning yourself with things that are beyond your control steers you away from doing a touch-up in your life. Construction workers know the meaning of touch-up all too well. They touch-up materials, surfaces and building construction on a consistent basis. It doesn't necessarily mean it will cost an arm and a foot to touch something up. When your life is touched up just a tad bit, you will begin to see the change in the specific areas in your life that operates better. I remember when I used to job hunt but never really followed up on the job or even visited the job of interest to show them that I am serious about working for them.

BUT…… MY HAIR ISN'T DONE!!

One day the light bulb went off and I asked myself what could I be doing different to at least get a call back? How can I be different from the average applicant? I began to read articles and look at videos to get some ideas and they worked. I received at least 3-4 job offers a month.

This is a numbers game as we know it. There is power in numbers. To get things to manifest in your life could be as easy as getting one other person beside yourself to believe in you and what you are doing. In my job hunt I called on my big sis to let her know what I was doing and what my job hunting goals were. She agreed with me, the 9-5 I will have will be a job that I want. That did manifest, but I also still invest in my gifts from God.

Operating outside of the four walls and thinking outside the box touch up your life drastically. For instance, instead of constantly texting the same people about the books that I wrote I began to do videos on how to write a book and how to move in the direction of writing.

This is not to say that letting people know about my book through text wasn't beneficial, but going the extra mile on what I believe in is never a waste of time. Being open to new things like meeting new people, going new places, and dabbling in new activities causes the universe to open more opportunities for you.

I know a lot of people that receive more if they are willing to just switch up their routine a little bit. The wrong thing to do is doubt the power that is within you. Let's big picture this touching thing up in your life thing for a minute. Years ago, I was given a prophecy about me writing a book. I didn't seek God first only people's approval.

This caused a major delay in me getting my book out. To make a long story short I began to seek the Holy Spirit on every detail of my first book then executed the entire project without turmoil. The common denominator here isn't how many books do I sell, but did I do what GOD told me to do. That is what real winners are about. Don't let the star stricken world fool you. No one really has it all together because we are all a work in progress.

Can you imagine going through your entire life not tapping into your real purpose or not even coming close to it? Often time's disappointments cause so much anger that the desire to help others is not even a part of our agenda. I for one had something else on my agenda when GOD began to show me that I didn't have the confidence to do much of anything. Have you noticed that the very thing that you have helped others achieve may have been a sprinkle of what you had challenges in? I started to question GOD about not having confidence but he said, "I am healing you while you are writing this book because you are willing to take yourself out of the equation to fulfill my purpose".

    I held back on a lot of things just because I wanted to know upfront how others would feel about what I am doing. I just heard a live video feed about not being sociable because it may just not be in you to be sociable. In laments term the quickest way to get to the top is to network. This great leader began to go on about how the disconnect or a relationship hindrance that they never had with their father caused them to actually be this way.

BUT…… MY HAIR ISN'T DONE!!

Your father and your mother are the first people primarily to accept you, so if they don't pump you up then there is a big chance that you will always look for the approval from other people. Perhaps they were never pumped up so that doesn't really resonate with them to give you the props that you actually need.

This is set up from GOD because a lot of times people encounter a true experience with him through other people. I believe throughout my life I have been very transparent. This includes admitting when I am wrong, admitting to hurt, guilt, any my imperfections.

As I steered away from doing everything average I began to see my life head in the directions exactly like my dreams. This is one of the reasons being traditional strikes boredom in me. Doing things differently can keep you from being jealous of the next person. What do I mean? Well moving out of your safe zone wipes off all confusion, and then you will begin to see the beauty in your life. Did I just say beauty? Yes. Your life is beautiful because no one else will ever be you. Even the people that are cloned will never really be themselves twice.

Can't and won't happen. This is not to say you won't have spiritual experiences, but GOD made each and every one of us with no mistakes. Finding out what you are good at improves your life to an extent that is above the clouds. I hear a lot of people saying they are good at so many things but they fear lack so they stay in the familiar. Trust me I used to be guilty of this. I wanted to always be comfortable and never inconvenienced.

I went to get my nails done today and I usually prefer a female to do them. I have

BUT…… MY HAIR ISN'T DONE!!

nothing against males doing my nails it's just what I prefer. There were no other nail techs available so I either had to wait for about 30 minutes or leave and come back on a busy day of mines during the week or let him do my nails. I decided to let the male do them. I was proud to step out of my comfort zone.

    I was basing a past experience and moving them over to a current event. Needless to say, he did a good job, so I even asked him to polish my toes. Life is nothing more than experiences and real stories and it basically boils down to which stories we want to keep private and which ones we want to share. I remember it was so hard adjusting to being a new mom because I was used to going out, doing this, doing that, and just being alone whenever I wanted to. True enough that when your life enhances the people that are supposed to be there will be and the ones that could have been for a season in your life is now gone.

Don't feel bad because some of the best roads were taken alone. For example, some people may not bungee jump or sky dive and this could be because of their fear of heights or just a choice not to do it. Either way doing what most people won't to have a life set up like most people will probably never have, is not a bad goal to have. What I see most of is people making it to what they fathom is their top, only to not pull anyone up with them.

A trainer once told the class to try everything one time. For me, river rafting, zip-lining, and deep-sea diving are certainly on my to-do list. As I close out this chapter while gazing out the window as I get a glimpse of the snow, I began to think about the grass underneath it. Why? Is it really suffering or just resting, this is what I am asking myself.

What we may think is an inconvenience, others may see it as a caution light. What does this mean for you? Glad you asked. When a person decides to no longer pursue what keeps them on fire it is the same thing as telling "GOD" I don't want to do what you created me to do".

If we truly knew the story behind the success of others then that is when we would start editing the pages of our lives. Life is like a vacation spot…we are just passing through and it is up to each person what they decide to do with it.

Touching up your life is easy or hard as you possess it to be
~Author, Veleta Jones~

Chapter 6-The Big Chop

Affirmation: I attract great things and people in my life

So... you just logged into your email account and for some odd reason the password is not working. Then you go on to keep trying the password you were for sure was the same password you used the last time you logged in. The only thing is now you are locked out and must use a password that you have not used before. It's almost like the email provider doesn't even want you to even come close to your old password. Now you must add a number and a special character to it as the log in credentials.

You then change it only to still come close to what you had. The email provider then sends you a log in security measure just to be sure your account is not hacked. Sounds like the

BUT…… MY HAIR ISN'T DONE!!

story of someone's life, right? Well maybe or maybe not. Bottom line is, it is only for your good that the password needs to be different then your old password. But, I will tell you this... resetting things in your life can bring what was dead back to life.

    The thing is that when something is dead in your life it can make people feel heavy, not resourceful, and quite frankly they may even feel left out from the crowd so-to-speak. The beauty of things that no longer gives you life, GOD might eventually cut that thing or someone out of your life. Often times we don't see what is not good for us so we continue to feed it or even the situation, and it's still malnourished.

    Even grass knows the difference between seasons which is why it cuts fall and winter off when it is time to do so without hesitation. For the ones that still treat their grass off season kudos to you for thinking outside the box.

I remember when I cut my hair completely off and I wanted to keep the hair that was cut in a bag. I never looked beyond the fact that the hair that was cut off will never be able to particularly grow back with that specific hair. This same scenario can apply to letting some people that is no good for you. This is not to say that everyone will need to cut out of your life, but some need to be simply looked at in their eyes and tell them "Look, this is how it is going to be". I have found that there is more respect when it is handled like that.

I notice in conversations that some people agree with certain things or tell you what you what they think you want to hear just to hurry up and finish talking to a person. There is popular saying for that "When life gives you lemons, make lemonade".

Sometimes it is not that simple to everyone due to the perception of a situation. As I begin to write this chapter I have some things to chop out of my life as well. Nothing is perfect, but can you admit that when you alleviate what kills your vibe you truly start to manifest what is for you. So, what is the big chop about, and how can it benefit you? Cutting down a big tree in your yard? Chopping up collard greens for Sunday dinner or even changing your circle?

Changing your circle could be hard to do because staying where you are can sometimes be your comfort zone. For instance, have you ever seen someone in passing whom you have not seen in years? I am sure we all have. Then usually by the end of the conversation numbers get exchanged and a "let's hang out soon open-ended statement is made. Rekindling with some people from your past is not necessarily a bad thing, but it could be a specific reason why you have not been in contact with an individual. Being confident can be simply saying "let's hang out right now".

As for me ever since high school I never really felt I fit in with certain people so, for some reason I have always had a small circle. Some say people with small circles are possibly loners or impatient with people. I disagree because sometimes your space is designated only for certain people.

I have finally divorced fear, doubt, pettiness, and several other things, and since then I have healed in so many areas of my life. I remember I applied for 101 jobs in approximately 45 days because I was so eager to get back out in the workforce. When you have a goal, and are focused you are willing to let go of whatever you need to in order to succeed. I ended up landing a job I applied for some years back. If I would have allowed some people to discourage me from handling my business the outcome would have been different.

Along the way you may notice that some people won't join your yellow brick road commute simply because they don't see your vision and frankly they don't have any business about themselves… so, why would they ultimately care about what you have going on.

I would not necessarily say I cut some people from my circles but, I will say that their vibe didn't rock with mines so I keep the ones close to me that enhanced my vibe.

BUT...... MY HAIR ISN'T DONE!!

Going back to the drawing board can keep you on the up and up when it comes to knowing what should or shouldn't be in your life.

     I remember taking plenty of breaks from social media, people, things that didn't value me, and electronics. I found out a lot about myself in that down time. Let's face it, some people may never get to a place where they can possibly be, because they are comfortable with keeping dead weight around them.

     Accepting the norm and what other people say is good for you is a big "No No," and failure could be knocking at your door. I discuss in a book I am featured in how it took me forever to even start writing books. Listening to other people say "Oh this will not work for you and why are you doing this, that and the other". I am so glad I did not focus on what people were saying and kept going. God is funny because he has a way of removing things out of your life in the blink of an eye.

At a former job I wanted to go to lunch at a certain time to converse how I felt I needed to, but it wasn't a bad thing to end up with a lunch or a break when general population was eating; I felt out of place. I eventually got used to it and started focusing on some things I wanted to accomplish in life. For instance, I used to write book chapters on my lunch break. I simple can tell in an instance what is for me.

At one point in my life I had 3 jobs in one year. Maybe because I didn't read the fine print of the job description or I didn't like the demeanor of the company's leaders. Being a leader myself, I don't allow people to treat me just any kind of way. It's not about being cocky, but about being confident in who you are.

BUT…… MY HAIR ISN'T DONE!!

Chopping yourself out of the way can simultaneously engulf enormous blessings on your life.

That thing that you want is out there right at your fingertips. Don't let something that should not be in your life keep you from the things that would love to be in your life, you know overflow, favor, wealth, peace, faith, and joy. Everything that is understood does not have to be explained unless you are a writer. LOL.

BUT…… MY HAIR ISN'T DONE!!

When the student is ready, the teacher will show up
~Author Unknown~

BUT…… MY HAIR ISN'T DONE!!

From the author's desk

So, now that you have learned that you are custom made and will not have any excuses going forward when allowing confidence to take over. While possessing positive thoughts and keeping a sound mind, just know oppositions will happen over and over, and your response will be the key holder. You are the driver behind the wheel of your life and God is all of the other parts so to speak. As I mentioned earlier God has already set aside the best life for you. Go Knock 'em dead!

If God can take my confidence to the next level then he will do it for you.
I have no doubt in my mind that after reading this book you will gain the confidence needed to take your life to the next level and receive everything that God have laid out for you.

BUT…… MY HAIR ISN'T DONE!!

Tis the season of no longer just saying what you are going to accomplish to actually executing your goals immediately. Don't be afraid of failing be afraid of not even trying.

Stay tuned for community events!

I would love the opportunity to connect with you.
Follow me on Instagram @konfidentagent
Email ~ konfidentchix@gmail.com
Website~ kisforkonfident.online
Facebook~ Veleta Jones

ABOUT THE AUTHOR

VELETA J. IS FROM ATLANTA, GA. AND HOLDS A B.A. DEGREE IN BUSINESS MANAGEMENT W/ A MINOR IN HUMAN RESOURCE MANAGEMENT AND HAS AUTHORED 5 PUBLISHED BOOKS- FIVE LAYERS DEEP ON HOW TO FORGIVE, S.M.RAMSEY-LIES, DECEPTION AND TRUTH, BEHIND THE SCENCES:CORPORATE AMERICA,CO-AUTHORED GLAMBITIOUS GUIDE TO GREATNESS AND THIS GEM YOU ARE NOW HOLDING IN YOUR HAND. SHE SERVED THREE YEARS AS ONE OF THE DIRECTORS OVER A MARRIAGE MINISTRY. SHE WORKED IN CORPORATE AMERICA FOR MANY YEARS. IN 2011 SHE RECEIVED A PERSONAL PROPHECY TO WRITE A BOOK NOT KNOWING THAT THERE ARE STEPS TO ACTUALLY RECEIVING A PROPHECY AND ACTUALLY BRINGING IT TO PASS.

BUT...... MY HAIR ISN'T DONE!!

NEEDLESS TO SAY, THAT PROPHECY CAME TO PASS 2 YEARS LATER. SHE STARTED HER ENTREPRENEURIAL JOURNEY IN 2013. SHE HAS OWNED OVER 4 BUSINESSES INCLUDING A JEWELRY COMPANY AND 3 NETWORK MARKETING COMPANIES. NOT THAT ANY OF THE BUSINESSES FAILED BUT ALL OF THEM INTRODUCED VELETA TO HER GOD-GIVEN TALENT OF WRITING. VELETA HAS ASSISTED WITH GHOSTWRITING THREE BOOKS AND HELD MANY COACHING SESSIONS ON HOW TO OVERCOME THE FEAR OF WRITING BOOKS SHE NOW HELPS OTHERS ALL AROUND THE GLOBE TO LEVEL UP IN THEIR CONFIDENCE...
FOR NEXT LEVEL ASSISTANCE IN A BOOST OF CONFIDENCE IN YOU LIFE, BOOK COACHING, RESUME FACE LIFTS, BOOK ORDERING, BOOKINGS, COLLABORATIONS PLEASE VISIT: KISFORKONFIDENT.ONLINE

www.ingramcontent.com/pod-product-compliance
Lightning Source LLC
LaVergne TN
LVHW051157080426
835508LV00021B/2676